I Take My Toothbrush Everywhere I Go

Written by Sheila Burke

Illustrated by Conor Toland

STJ LLC (BOOK PUBLISHING)

Hyde Park, Massachusetts

I Take My Toothbrush Everywhere I Go
Published by STJ LLC (Book Publishing)
Boston, Massachusetts
sewb59@yahoo.com

Sheila Burke, Publisher & Editorial Director
QualityPress.info, Book Packager
Conor Toland, Illustrator

STJ LLC Books are available at special discounts for bulk purchases, sales promotions, fund raising or educational purposes.

JJ loved his toothbrush so much that he took it everywhere he went.

1

He took it to breakfast.

He took it to school.

And he even took it to the park.

He took it up to the sky

and down to the ground.

Around and around his toothbrush went.

JJ knew the importance of brushing his teeth after each meal, morning, noon, and night.

Swish, swish, swoosh! Up and down and all around.

8

JJ loved his toothbrush so much that he took it everywhere he went.

9

He even took it to his visit with Nana.

Nana gave JJ a great big hug.

JJ didn't even notice his toothbrush fell on the floor.

Nana and JJ sat down to eat and talk about what's been going on.

After eating, JJ went
to brush his teeth.

He looked in his backpack to get his toothbrush but it was gone!

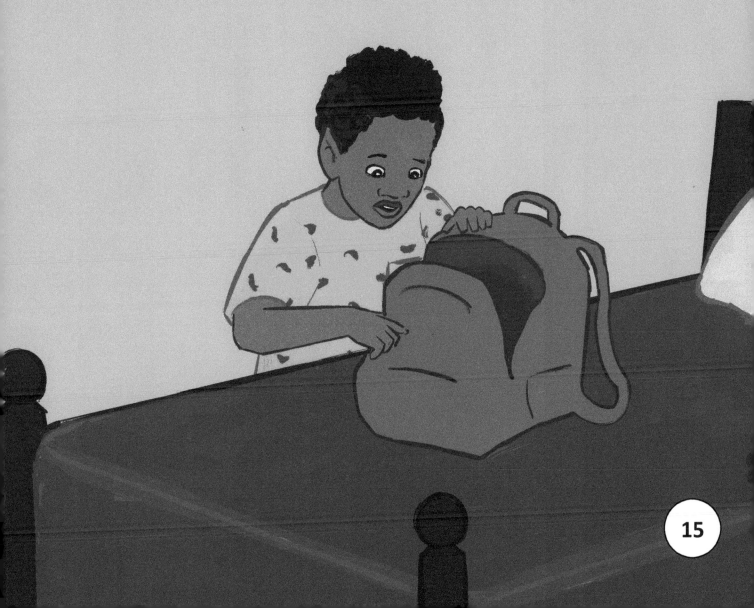

He looked on top of
the bed and under.

JJ yelled, "Nana, it's gone!"

Nana ran upstairs
and asked,
"What's gone?"

18

JJ said, "My toothbrush is gone! I take my toothbrush everywhere I go."

19

Nana smiled, "Here it is! It fell out of your pocket when I gave you a great big hug!"

JJ said, "Thank you, Nana," with a big smile and gave her a hug.

ABOUT THE AUTHOR

Sheila Burke is a 61-year-old Female Author and Publisher of children's books. When Sheila is writing the books, her biggest inspirations come from her children and grandchildren, who are funny, witty, and full of surprises and aspirations.

I Take My Toothbrush Everywhere I Go is Sheila Burke's third book. Her first two books are JadyWady and the Bedbugs, JadyWady and the Birthday Surprise, and her 4th book is Polk-A-Dots and Stripes, ABC's.

In 2019 – Sheila Burke Produced a Documentary on BNN – TV "Around Town" on Boston's Homelessness Crisis due to "gentrification" and other issues and was selected and shown in the 2020 Roxbury International Film Festival (RIFF) https://vimeo.com/333239102

In 2016 – Sheila Burke Wrote and Produced the Animation of her first children's book Jady Wady and the Bedbugs and was selected and shown in the Roxbury International Film Festival (RIFF) https://vimeo.com/1590150905.

SHEILA'S DEDICATION & ACKNOWLEDGEMENTS

I Take My Toothbrush Everywhere I Go is dedicated to my 6-years-old grandson, Jaylen Amir Mathis, who is funny, intelligent and dear to my heart. Jaylan stayed overnight at my house and I said, "It's time to get ready for bed. Where is your toothbrush?" He said, "Here it is!" Nana, "I Take My Toothbrush Everywhere I Go"; and from there, this book was created. Thank you, JJ for your Inspiration, Wittiness, and Love.

Also, a great big "Thank You" to Conor Toland for doing amazing illustrations to enhance the story-telling.

9 781087 921440